animals
at
the 💙 zoo

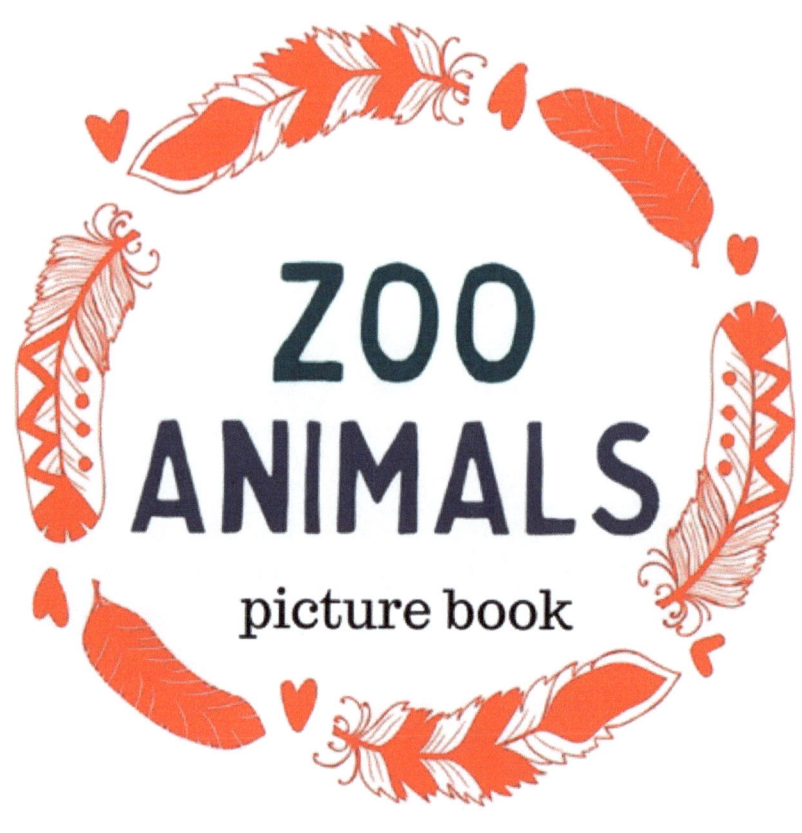

ZOO ANIMALS

picture book

WRITTEN AND ILLUSTRATED BY

Vanessa Lewis

Connect with Vanessa

Facebook- Vanessa Lewis Books

Email- vanessalewis8@gmail.com

If you enjoyed this book, please kindly leave a review to let others know what you think.

www.ingramcontent.com/pod-product-compliance
Lightning Source LLC
Chambersburg PA
CBHW050803290526
45792CB00008B/2304